Shocking Sharks

Charlotte Guillain

Raintree is an imprint of Capstone Global Library Limited, a company incorporated in England and Wales having its registered office at 7 Pilgrim Street, London, EC4V 6LB – Registered company number: 6695582

www.raintreepublishers.co.uk
myorders@raintreepublishers.co.uk

Text © Capstone Global Library Limited 2013
First published in hardback in 2013
Paperback edition first published in 2014
The moral rights of the proprietor have been asserted.

Edited by Daniel Nunn, Rebecca Rissman, and Catherine Veitch
Designed by Victoria Allen
Picture research by Mica Brancic
Production by Victoria Fitzgerald
Originated by Capstone Global Library Ltd
Printed and bound in China by CTPS

ISBN 978 1 406 26079 3 (hardback)
17 16 15 14 13
10 9 8 7 6 5 4 3 2 1

ISBN 978 1 406 26086 1 (paperback)
18 17 16 15 14
10 9 8 7 6 5 4 3 2 1

British Library Cataloguing in Publication Data
Guillain, Charlotte.
Shocking sharks. -- (Walk on the wild side)
597.3-dc23
A full catalogue record for this book is available from the British Library.

Acknowledgements
We would like to thank the following for permission to reproduce photographs: Corbis p. 22 (Minden Pictures/© Mike Parry); Getty Images p. 18 (Science Faction/Stephen Frink); Image Quest Marine p. 27 (V&W/Andy Murch); Nature Picture Library pp. 4 (2020VISION/© Alex Mustard), 5, 10, 12 (both © David Fleetham), 7, 13, 16, 17, 20 (all © Brandon Cole), 11(© Jeff Rotman), 14 (© Mark Carwardine), 15 (© Alex Mustard), 19, 21 (both © Doug Perrine), 23 (© Juan Carlos Munoz), 24 (© Jeff Rotman), 25, 28 (both © Juan Carlos Munoz), 29 (© Tony Heald); Shutterstock pp. 8 (© Natursports), 9 (© Senai Aksoy).

Cover photograph of a Great White Shark reproduced with permission of Getty Images (Visuals Unlimited, Inc./David Fleetham).

We would like to thank Michael Bright for his invaluable help in the preparation of this book.

Every effort has been made to contact copyright holders of material reproduced in this book. Any omissions will be rectified in subsequent printings if notice is given to the publisher.

Some words are shown in bold, **like this**. You can find out what they mean by looking in the glossary.

Contents

Introducing sharks

Sharks are known as deadly ocean hunters. There are around 450 **species** of shark, but very few ever attack humans. All sharks are a type of fish. Some are huge, such as the whale shark. Others are tiny.

Basking sharks feed on tiny sea creatures called **plankton**.

4

hammerhead
shark

Did you know?
Sharks have swum
in the oceans for
hundreds of millions
of years.

Where do sharks live?

Sharks live in oceans all around the world, but many **species** live in warm seas. Great white sharks are the biggest fish in the world to hunt and kill other animals. They are fearsome **predators**.

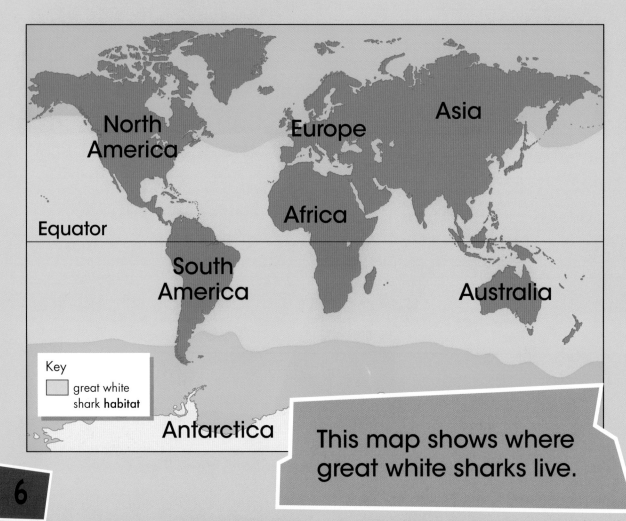

North America

Europe

Asia

Equator

Africa

South America

Australia

Key

great white shark **habitat**

Antarctica

This map shows where great white sharks live.

Great white sharks swim in seas all around the world.

What do sharks look like?

A shark has a **streamlined** body that helps it to swim quickly through the water. Sharks also have powerful tails that push them along at speed. They have fins to keep them balanced.

tail

fin

The fin on
a shark's back
is called the
dorsal fin.

dorsal fin

Terrifying teeth

Many sharks have sharp teeth in their mouths. There are several rows of teeth, and new teeth keep replacing old ones. A great white shark's teeth are **triangular**, with jagged edges to slash through **prey**.

Did you know?

A great white shark has around 300 teeth in its mouth!

Sharks' teeth can be 7.5 centimetres long.

Bite power!

Great white sharks have incredible biting power. Their jaws are extremely strong, pushing the sharp teeth into **prey** and tearing it apart. The shark's jaws are not connected to its skull. This means it can open them very wide as it moves in to bite prey.

Did you know?

Sharks don't chew their food. They swallow it whole!

Cunning camouflage

A great white shark's back is dark grey, so any **prey** looking down into the dark ocean from above will not see the shark. The shark's underside is white. Any prey looking up at the shark from below won't see it either. The white underside blends in with the light at the surface of the water.

shark's back

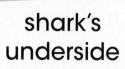

shark's underside

Hunting

Great white sharks are brilliant hunters. The shark **stalks**, or quietly follows, its **prey** from below or behind. The shark follows until its prey is close by and then attacks with a burst of speed.

Did you know?

When sharks attack, they can move at speeds of up to 50 kilometres per hour.

This shark twists its body as it turns tightly to race after its prey.

Smelling and hearing

Sharks have an incredible sense of smell. They can smell just one drop of blood in the water if an injured animal is nearby. Sharks also have a good sense of hearing, which helps them to find **prey**.

seal

shark

Did you know?

A great white shark
can even smell a
group of seals from
3 kilometres away!

Super senses

Sharks also have extra, super senses to help them find **prey**. Inside their **snouts** are special tubes that can feel **vibrations**, or movement, in the water made by their prey.

snout

Did you know?

Sharks also use their senses to help them find their way around as they swim.

Spyhopping

Great white sharks use **spyhopping** to look for **prey**. They stick their heads right out of the water and look around. Great white sharks can also jump right out of the water as they attack their prey.

When great white sharks jump out of the water like this, it is called **breaching**.

Keeping warm

Great white sharks are able to keep their bodies warmer than the water around them. They don't lose heat from their bodies into the sea. Keeping warm means a great white shark has the energy to swim after fast **prey** quickly when it needs to.

Baby sharks

Baby sharks are called pups. Mothers give birth to pups rather than laying eggs like other fish do. Great white sharks are born with a full set of teeth. They are immediately ready to swim away from their mother and start hunting!

Great white pups can be over 1.5 metres long when they are born.

baby mako shark

Life for a shark

Many people are afraid of sharks, but very few sharks attack humans. In fact, great white shark numbers are falling because people hunt them. Great white sharks are among the best hunters in the ocean, and people will always be amazed by this skilful **predator**.

Did you know?

Nobody knows how long great white sharks live for. Scientists think it's no more than 30 years.

Glossary

breaching when sharks jump out of the water

habitat natural home for an animal or a plant

plankton tiny animals and plants drifting in the ocean

predator animal that kills and eats other animals

prey animal killed by another animal for food

snout animal's nose

species type of animal

spyhopping when a shark lifts its head out of the water to look around

stalk hunt an animal quietly, trying to stay hidden

streamlined shaped to move easily through water or air

triangular shaped like a triangle

vibrations quick, shaking movement

Find out more

Books

Shark, Miranda MacQuitty (Dorling Kindersley, 2011)

Sharks, Catriona Clarke (Usborne, 2007)

Sharks, Valerie Bodden (Franklin Watts, 2012)

Shark vs. Killer Whale, Isabel Thomas (Raintree, 2006)

Websites

gowild.wwf.org.uk/regions/oceans-fact-files/basking-shark
Find out more about basking sharks on the WWF website.

kids.nationalgeographic.com/kids/animals/creaturefeature/great-white-shark/
You can learn about lots of different types of shark on the National Geographic website.

www.bbc.co.uk/nature/life/Great_white_shark
Watch videos of great white sharks in action on the BBC Nature website.

Index